The Waking Nightmare :

The Russian Sleep Experiment

Cellier Marvin

Copyright © 2024 Cellier Marvin
All rights reserved

SUMMARY

Chapter 1: The Icy Shadow of the KGB

Chapter 2: Whispers in the Dark

Chapter 3: The Dance of the Awakened Demons

Chapter 4: The Powerless Guardians

Chapter 5: Shadows of Experience

Chapter 6: The Fractures of Reality

Chapter 7: The Gates of Enlightenment

Conclusion: The Awakened Nightmare - The Russian Sleep Experiment

The Icy Shadow of the KGB

It was a time when the Soviet Union reigned in the shadow of the Iron Curtain, an era where paranoia and secrecy were the currency of power. At the heart of this political spider web, hidden in the vast frozen expanses of Russia, was a research complex shrouded in a sinister aura. It was here, in the clandestine laboratories of the KGB, that the horrifying story of "The Russian Sleep Experiment" was born.

The walls of this complex were impregnated with the biting cold of isolation, while scientists worked in the shadows, manipulating the threads of the experiment with icy indifference. The room of experience, a concrete cube without windows, stood like a silent grave within this austere establishment.

The protagonists of this experience were political prisoners, souls condemned to oblivion, chosen to serve as guinea pigs in this perverse quest to understand the mysteries of the human psyche.

These prisoners, already broken by the chains of injustice, would become the subjects of unimaginable horror.

The complex was imbued with an ethereal atmosphere, where the stifled murmurs of scientists mingled with the roar of machines. The dark corridors resounded with hushed steps and locked doors, creating a sinister symphony that set the stage for the inhumane experience that would follow.

It was in this place that the first notes of the history of the Russian sleep experiment were written, as scientists plunged into the abyssal darkness of the secrets of the human mind. It was the beginning of a tragedy that would leave an indelible scar on the fabric of reality, a story that would transcend the limits of comprehension and haunt the dark pages of history.

The Whispers in the Dark

During the late 1940s, Russian researchers kept five people awake for a fortnight using an experimental stimulant-based gas.

They were locked in a sealed environment in order to control their oxygen consumption so that the gas would not kill them, since it was toxic from a high concentration.
This took place before the invention of closed-circuit cameras, so they only had microphones and glass windows a dozen centimeters thick in the shape of a porthole that allowed them to be monitored.

The room was equipped with extra beds without bedding, running water and toilets, and contained books and enough dry food so that they could hold five for more than a month.

The Awakened Nightmare :
The Russian Sleep Experiment

The test subjects were political prisoners deemed enemies of the state during the Second World War.

Everything went well for the first five days; the subjects rarely complained, for they had been promised that they would be free if they agreed to undergo the test and not sleep for thirty days (although release was out of the question).

Their conversations and activities were monitored, and it was noted that they were only talking about increasingly traumatic incidents in their past, with the tone of the conversation becoming much darker after the fourth day.

After five days, they began to complain about the circumstances and events that had led them to where they were and to show signs of severe paranoia. They stopped talking to each other and instead started talking to microphones or to one-way mirrors from the portholes. Curiously, they seemed to think they could gain the confidence of the experimenters by turning against their comrades, the other test subjects in captivity with them.

The researchers initially assumed it was a gas effect.

The Awakened Nightmare:
The Russian Sleep Experiment

The Dance of the Awakened Demons

After nine days, the first of them began to scream. He ran the length of the chamber screaming at the top of his lungs for three hours without stopping, and then tried not to stop, but he could only occasionally produce small squeaks.
The researchers thought he tore his vocal cords.

The most surprising thing about this behaviour is how the other subjects reacted… or rather did not.
They continued to whisper to the attention of the microphones until the second the screams began.

Two of the silent captives then boned the books, coated all the pages with their own excrement and stuck them on the glass of the portholes.

The screams quickly stopped.

The Awakened Nightmare:
The Russian Sleep Experiment

The whispers addressed to the microphones also.

Three days have passed. The researchers checked the microphones every hour to make sure they were working because they thought it was impossible for five people locked in a room to produce no sound.

Oxygen consumption in the chamber indicated that all five of them must be alive. In fact, it was the amount of oxygen that five people would consume during extremely strenuous exercise.

On the morning of the fourteenth day, the researchers did something they had said they would not do to get a reaction from the captives: they used the intercom of the room, hoping to provoke any response from the detainees.
They were afraid that they were dead or in a vegetative state.

They said, "We'll open the room to test the microphones; stay away from the door and lie on your stomach on the floor, or you'll be shot.
If you follow these rules, one of you will gain his freedom."

To their surprise, they heard a single sentence uttered in a calm voice: "We no longer want to be released."

The Powerless Guardians

Debates broke out between the researchers and the military forces that funded the project. Since it was impossible to obtain other answers using the intercom, it was finally decided that the door to the room would be open at midnight on the fifteenth day.

The chamber was emptied of stimulating gas and filled with fresh air, and voices from the microphones immediately began to protest.

Three different voices began to beg, as if the life of their life's love was at stake, to turn the gas on.
The chamber was opened and soldiers were sent inside to find the test subjects. They started screaming louder than ever, and the soldiers quickly did the same when they saw what was inside.

Four of the five subjects were still alive, although the state in which they were not qualified as «alive».

The Awakened Nightmare :
The Russian Sleep Experiment

Food rations from the previous five days had not been affected. There were pieces of flesh from the dead subject's thighs and torso embedded in the drain in the center of the chamber, clogging it, and allowing about ten centimeters of water to accumulate on the floor.

The portion of this water that was composed of blood was not determined. The four "surviving" subjects also had large portions of muscle and skin removed from their bodies. The destruction of the flesh and bones in the open on their fingers indicated that the wounds had been inflicted on the hand, not with the teeth, as the researchers had initially thought.

More precise observations of the position and angle of injuries showed that most, if not all, injuries were self-inflicted.

The abdominal organs under the ribcage of the four subjects had been removed. While the heart, lungs, and diaphragm had remained in place, the skin and most of the muscles attached to the ribs had been torn away, making it possible to distinguish the lungs through the ribs. All the blood vessels and organs were intact, they had simply been removed and placed on the ground, distributed around eviscerated bodies, but still alive, subjects.

The digestive system of the four subjects could be observed in operation, digesting food. It was very soon clear that they were digesting their own flesh, that they had ripped out and devoured during the previous days.

Most of the soldiers were Russians from a special commando assigned to the facility, but most refused to return to the room to take out the test subjects. They kept screaming for them to be left in the room and begging for the gas to be turned back so they wouldn't fall asleep.

To everyone's surprise, the subjects fought violently when they were released. One of the Russian soldiers had his throat torn and died, another one came out seriously injured, after having his testicles ripped and perforated an artery of one of his legs by the teeth of a subject. Five other soldiers lost their lives, including those who committed suicide in the weeks following the incident.

During the fight, the spleen of one of the living subjects ruptured and he bled out almost immediately. Medical researchers tried to put him to sleep, but it proved useless.

The Awakened Nightmare : The Russian Sleep Experiment

The Shadows of the Experience

He was injected more than ten times the maximum dose for a human of a morphine derivative, and he continued to fight like a rabid animal, breaking the ribs and arms of one of the doctors. It was found that the heart continued to beat for two full minutes after the bleeding brought it to a point where its vascular system was filled with more air than blood.

Even after he stopped, he continued to scream for three minutes, striving to attack anyone who came within range and continually repeating the word "MORE", increasingly weakly, until he was silenced.

The three surviving test subjects were immobilized and transported to a medical facility, both with their vocal cords still intact, continuing to beg the return of the gas to stay awake…

The Awakened Nightmare:
The Russian Sleep Experiment

The three with the most injuries were taken to the only operating theatre in the facility.
During the procedure to prepare him for the replacement of his internal organs, he proved immune to the sedatives that were administered to him in order to put him in condition for surgery.

He was furiously struggling against his bonds when the anesthetic gas was brought in to put him out of action.
He managed to tear through almost all of a ten-centimeter thick leather band attached to one of his wrists, even with the weight of a ninety-kilogram soldier trying to hold that wrist still. A just above normal amount was needed to put him to sleep, and the second his eyelids closed, his heart stopped.

During the autopsy of the test subject who died on the operating table, it was revealed that his blood contained three times the normal oxygen concentration. The muscles that were still attached to his skeleton were horribly jagged and he had broken nine bones in his struggle for control.

Mostly because of the strength that his own muscles had exerted on them.

The Fractures of the Reality

The second survivor was the first in the group to start shouting. With his vocal cords destroyed, he was unable to beg or protest the operation, and he only reacted by shaking his head violently to show his disapproval when the anesthetic gas was brought near him. He shook his head to say yes when someone reluctantly suggested trying the operation without anesthesia, and did not react for the six hours it took to replace his abdominal organs and cover them with what was left of his skin.

The surgeon presiding over the procedure kept repeating that it should be medically impossible for the subject to be alive. A terrified nurse attending the operation said she had seen the patient's mouth smile several times, each time her eyes crossed hers.

The Awakened Nightmare: The Russian Sleep Experiment

When the surgery ended, the subject looked at the surgeon and began to whistle strongly, trying to talk while struggling. Assuming it was important, the surgeon asked for a pencil and notebook so the patient could write his message.

It was simple. "Keep cutting."

The other two test subjects underwent the same procedure, both without anesthesia. However, it was necessary to inject them with a paralytic during the operation.
The surgeon could not perform the surgery while the patients were laughing continuously.

Once paralyzed, subjects could only follow the doctors' eyes. The paralytic was eliminated from their system after an abnormally short period and they quickly tried to escape.

By the time they could start talking again, they started asking for the stimulating gas again. The researchers tried to ask them why they had inflicted these wounds on themselves, why they had ripped out their own entrails and why they wanted the gas again.

The only answer was, "I have to stay awake."

The Awakened Nightmare:
The Russian Sleep Experiment

The links of the three subjects were strengthened and they were put back in the room while waiting to know what was going to be done with them. The researchers, facing the anger of the military «benefactors» because of their inability to achieve the goal they had set for them, thought of euthanasia. The commanding officer, a former KGB agent, instead saw potential in them, and wanted to see what would happen if they were plunged back into the gas.

The researchers formally opposed it, but their objections were ignored.

In order to prepare them to be sealed again in the chamber, the subjects were connected to an electroencephalographic monitor, and their bonds were strengthened for long-term containment. To everyone's surprise, the three of them stopped struggling when someone let it slip that they were going to go back into the gas. It was obvious that at the time, they were having a hard time staying awake. One of the subjects who could speak hummed loudly and without stopping; the mute subject pressed his legs with all his might, first the right, then the left, then again the right, in order to have something to concentrate on.

The last subject kept his head above his pillow and blinked quickly.

The Awakened Nightmare :
The Russian Sleep Experiment

The Gates of the Awakening

Having been the first to be linked to the electroencephalogram, most researchers observed its brainwaves with surprise.

They were normal most of the time, but sometimes displayed a simple line. It was as if he suffered several brain deaths, before everything became normal again. As they focused on the paper coming out of the monitor, only one nurse saw her eyelids close as her head fell back on her pillow. His brainwaves immediately mutated into those of deep sleep, then the straight line appeared for the last time, as his heart stopped.

The only subject remaining in a state of speaking began to shout to be sealed immediately. His brain waves showed the same straight lines as the one who died after falling asleep. The commander gave the order to seal the chamber with the two subjects inside, as well as three researchers.

The Awakened Nightmare :
The Russian Sleep Experiment

He then pointed his weapon at the remaining subject, still tied to the bed while the remaining members of the medical and research team fled the room. "I won't be locked in there with these things! Not with you," he shouted to the man at the table.

WHAT ARE YOU? he asked. I need to know!"

Subject smiled.

"Did you forget so easily?" replied the subject. "We are you. We are the madness that is hidden in each of you, begging to be liberated at any time in your animal mind. We are what you hide every night in your beds. We are what you silence and paralyze when you reach the night paradise that we cannot walk."

The researcher stopped. Then he aimed at the heart of the subject and fired. The electroencephalogram then displayed a straight line, while the subject choked, weakly letting out a few words: "If… close to being…free…"

Conclusion : The Waking Nightmare - The Russian Sleep Experiment

The silent laboratory still echoes the weight of the released darkness, a sinister echo of the Russian experiment on sleep that haunts memories.
This waking nightmare, orchestrated in the meanders of the KGB, left behind a terrifying picture of the human soul pushed to its darkest limits.

The subjects, once men, have been transformed into wandering vestiges of their humanity, prisoners of the unspeakable shadows that still haunt them.
The helpless guardians, witnesses of this descent into hell, bear the burden of distorted murmurs and insane laughter, a burden that has eroded their own reality.

The shadows of the experience persist, extending beyond the walls of the laboratory, sneaking into the darkest corners of the collective unconscious. The waking nightmare insinuated itself into the minds of the witnesses, leaving behind an indelible psychic scar.

The Awakened Nightmare : The Russian Sleep Experiment

The Russian sleep experiment remains as a macabre warning about the limits of the human quest to unravel the mysteries of the psyche. It resounds like a sinister echo, recalling that sometimes, in the search for knowledge, the human mind can become the playground of dark forces, releasing unspeakable horrors.

The waking nightmare persists, a dark chapter in human history, recalling that even in the icy darkness of research, there are lines that man should never cross.

The Russian experiment on sleep, a terrible tragedy, stands as a gloomy warning in the great book of the horrors of humanity, a story whose shadows will continue to haunt dreams and nightmares, long after the lab lights went out.

Printed in Dunstable, United Kingdom